From Flea Market to Fabulous

Kerry Trout

NORTH LIGHT BOOKS

CINCINNATI, OHIO

www.nlbooks.com

About the Author

Kerry Trout is a self-taught artist who has been painting all her life. She considers her talent a gift, crediting it greatly to inheriting her mother's artistic genes. She enjoys rendering subjects in acrylics, gouache or pastels, and has painted on every surface imaginable. She paints decorative furniture from her Indiana studio, and teaches her techniques to local students. When not painting she writes books, magazine articles, and designs pattern packets. She is a member of the Society of Decorative Painters and a Helping Artist for DecoArt. In her spare time she enjoys antiquing, genealogy, and camping and fishing with husband Tom and their miniature dachshund, Heidi. You may view her portfolio by visiting www.kerrytrout.com, and you can write to Kerry at P.O. Box 125, Danville, IN 46122.

From Flea Market to Fabulous. Copyright © 2001 by Kerry Trout. Manufactured in China. All rights reserved. The patterns and drawings in this book are for the personal use of the decorative painter. By permission of the author and publisher, they may be either hand-traced or photocopied to make single copies, but under no circumstances may they be resold or republished. It is permissible for the purchaser to paint the designs contained herein and sell them at fairs, bazaars and craft shows. No other part of this book may be reproduced in any form or by any electronic or mechanical means including information storage and retrieval systems without permission in writing from the publisher, except by a reviewer, who may quote brief passages in a review. Published by North Light Books, an imprint of F&W Publications, Inc., 1507 Dana Avenue, Cincinnati, Ohio 45207. (800) 289-0963. First edition.

Other fine North Light Books are available from your local bookstore, art supply store or direct from the publisher.

05 04 03 02 01   5 4 3 2

Library of Congress Cataloging-in-Publication Data

Trout, Kerry
    From flea market to fabulous / Kerry Trout.—1st ed.
       p. cm.
    Includes index.
    ISBN 1-58180-091-6 (alk. paper)—ISBN 1-58180-092-4 (pbk. : alk. paper)
    1. Flea markets. I. Title.

    HF5482.15 .T76 2001
    381'.192—dc21   00-048708
                                                                                        CIP

Editor: Heather Dakota
Designer: Lisa Buchanan
Page Layout: Lisa Holstein
Production Coordinator: Sara Dumford
Photographer: Christine Polomsky

Metric conversion chart available on page 142.

Dedication

To my good friend Jean, who knew before I did that I could succeed; whose creative vision has helped me transform her flea market finds into painted furnishings for her home and garden. Her praise and encouragement is uplifting, and her zest unending. I hope to be as young when I'm eighty-four.

Acknowledgments

Special thanks to Heather Dakota for going above and beyond, and for her creative wisdom and unselfish advice; Kathy Kipp for her professionalism and kindness; and Christine Polomsky for anticipating my every need. These North Light ladies are a treat to work with.

Deep appreciation to my family: Dad and Jeannette for their constant love and encouragement; Bruce, Amy, Kathy and Beth for their great support — and simply being the finest brother and sisters anyone could want; my son Bobby, for his much-needed help in prepping some of the pieces in this book; and of course, Tom, my best friend.

I'd also like to thank the following people who contributed in different ways to the production of this book: Carolyn Cave, Anne Matthai, Sue Nadin, Rosemary Reynolds, Sharon Spencer.

The flea market scenes were photographed at the Burlington Flea Market in Burlington, Kentucky. Thanks to the following vendors for allowing us to take photographs in their booths: Tunnel Mill Antiques; Alice's Past to Present; Fred Watkins; Tommie Mitchell; Joyce Cox; and Bradley's Antiques.

Introduction

It really is true that one person's trash is another's treasure. The "junk" we amass in our basements, attics and garages attracts people like bees to honey once you put it out in the front yard! You never know what you'll find at a yard sale, and that's part of what makes the hunt so much fun for me. And with the collectibles craze at an all-time high, it's no wonder people flock to these sales every weekend.

Whether it's advertised as a garage sale, rummage sale, or flea market, it's basically the same thing and it's a great place to find bargains. But how many times have you seen a thingamajig at a sale and asked, "What would I do with this?"

Well, to the decorative artist, many of these common flea market finds — although plain and even ugly from the start — can offer a vast array of paintable surfaces.

This book is the result of just one trip to an outdoor flea market. I bought ten items you would typically find for sale at a flea market, and transformed each one into something special and unique. With my easy directions and step-by-step photos, you too can turn someone else's trash into your own hand-painted treasure!

Table of Contents

PROJECT 1

From Old Fruit Crates to Decorative Display Boxes

page 12

PROJECT 2

From Old Milk Can to Fantastic Farm Scene

page 24

PROJECT 6

From Smoking Stand to Nest of Chickens

page 66

PROJECT 7

From Broken Table to Faux Delft Tiles

page 84

Finding the "Good Stuff" at the Flea Market

Things you need to know before going to a yard sale or flea market

✓ Sometimes the newspaper ad for a yard sale will include the phone number. Take advantage of it. Call and ask to preview the sale the day before. Some people will allow you to come over if it means unloading their unwanted items.

✓ Wear a fanny pack or money belt instead of carrying a purse. Take plenty of cash in denominations of one and five dollar bills only. If you offer eight dollars for a ten-dollar item, you won't want to pay with a twenty.

✓ Start out early in the day. The best finds are snatched up quickly. But if a yard sale ad says "No early birds," don't arrive before the advertised time.

✓ Take a van or truck if available. You don't want to pass up a great headboard because you don't have a way to get it home.

✓ Take friends with you. It's more fun and you'll have help carrying your goodies. A wagon is also a handy item for holding your purchases at a large flea market.

✓ Everything is negotiable, especially at flea markets. When you find something you want, make it obvious to the vendor, but tell him the cost is a bit more than you wanted to pay. Ask if that's the best he can do. If he won't budge on the price, put it back and walk away. More than likely he'll have a change of heart. Without insulting him, you can also point out damage or defects.

✓ When you see something you absolutely must have, pick it up right then. If you don't, it will surely be snatched up by the next person. If it's a large piece, such as furniture, lay your hands on it until you get the vendor's attention or take the price tag off the piece and go to him. Most people won't give an item without a price tag a second look.

Inspect all sides of a piece of furniture. This piece was impressive until I opened the door and it nearly fell off in my hands.

This bench had an appealing shape, but was too far gone to consider for painting. The wood was split and the entire piece wobbled.

This little sleigh would have made a beautiful painting project, but there was nothing little about the price.

Pull out all of the drawers and check the construction. Dove-tailed joints are signs of a well-made piece and contribute to its sturdiness.

The paneled doors on this cabinet are what caught my eye. They can be lots of fun to paint. But this piece was made to look like an antique, even down to the fake teeth marks, normally made by a rat. Unless the piece has a really good price on it, beware of reproductions.

This old European wagon could make a charming project, but its crude construction and worn finish make it a primitive. It was priced as such.

Check the sturdiness of a wooden chair by grasping the back and the seat as pictured, and trying to move them in opposite directions. A strong, sound chair should have no play or give in the movement.

Some things you don't dare repaint, but simply appreciate. This cabinet was painted over a hundred years ago by another decorative artist.

Normally, you don't want to use a primitive piece of furniture for a painting project. It's best to retain the original finish. In this case, the outside of the cabinet had been stripped and sanded, reducing its value considerably. This makes it perfect for painting.

Kerosene heaters seem to pop up at every sale I go to. Ten dollars was a bargain for this one, and I knew exactly what I was going to do with it (see page 56).

Picnic baskets are easy to find, and almost all of them have wooden lids that are perfect for painting. Baskets are typically fragile, so make sure you inspect all sides before buying one.

Galvanized metal tubs, buckets and watering cans are plentiful at flea markets. Wouldn't this make a great planter? (See page 48.)

This little cradle was handsomely painted with folk art strokework and heavily antiqued to look very old. We had to inspect it closely to tell whether or not it was old. It was not sold as an antique, and I admire the artist whose work looked so convincing.

The crackled and weathered finish on this old counter is original and sought after today—thus the reason for the exorbitant price. (Hint: You can make your own crackled and weathered finish! See Project 7, Faux Delft Tiles.)

Supplies Needed

Prepping Supplies

It is important to properly prepare your flea market finds before painting them. These supplies will help you prepare each piece and protect the wonderful painting you'll be adding. Each project in this book gives specific prepping instructions.

- Drop cloth
- Sanding sponge
- Tack cloth
- Primer (such as Kilz or BIN)

Miscellaneous Painting Supplies

These supplies will make your work a lot cleaner and easier to do.

- 2-inch natural bristle brush
- 2-inch foam brush
- White chalk pencil
- White and black transfer paper
- Tracing paper
- Paper towels
- Sea sponge
- Latex gloves
- Painter's tape (low tack)
- T-square
- Straightedge
- Water basin

Brushes

Any artist will tell you that nothing contributes more to a successful painting than good quality brushes. If the brushes you have lose bristles, throw them away and buy the best brushes you can afford.

The projects in this book call for a variety of brush types and sizes, a few of which are shown here. The painting instructions for each project list the brushes you'll need.

Paints and Mediums

Your local craft store stocks the paints and special mediums used in this book. I use only acrylic paints, which are widely available in handy 2-oz. squeeze bottles. Some of the most popular colors also come in a money-saving 8-oz. size. If there is no craft store near you, you can also locate distributors through mail order catalogs and on the Internet.

For the projects in this book painted on metal surfaces, I used DecoArt's No-Prep Metal Paint, which also comes in 2-oz. squeeze bottles available at craft stores.

Brush 'n Blend Extender by DecoArt is a special medium that prolongs the drying time of acrylic paint. Dressing the corner of the brush with it before loading with paint will allow more open time and make it easier to blend colors.

DecoArt also has a new line of self-sealing paints for use on larger surfaces and furniture called

Americana Satins. These come in a variety of colors and can be easily mixed to achieve more shades.

Antiquing gels come in only a handful of colors, so if you need something different, DecoArt has a Clear Gel Stain. Just mix it with your acrylic paint to achieve the desired shade of antiquing.

There are a few porcelain crackles on the market, but I prefer the one made by Valspar Decorative Effects. Don't confuse this crackle glaze with Weathered

Wood Crackle Medium—they produce entirely different crackled effects.

Finally, DecoArt's DuraClear Satin Varnish is an interior/exterior waterbase polyurethane I use after all painting is finished. It acts as a protective topcoat and brings out the intensity of acrylic colors. You can find it at any craft store.

From Old Fruit Crates to
Decorative
Display Boxes

These old wooden crates were in great shape and only $2 apiece! They were originally used to ship grapes (as the stamped-on graphics showed), and they are considerably smaller than a normal size fruit crate—making them so versatile.

I'm a sucker for old seed packets and can labels, and one of my favorite finds is an old paper label from a Trout (my last name) brand Fruit Growers crate. I really love the old graphics and bright colors. So when I found these crates, it seemed only natural to come up with some lively new "labels" for them. I bought an armload of them and immediately envisioned them holding hand towels, letters, potted plants and so on.

Paint one up and fill it with pretty napkins, gourmet jam and some fresh scones, and you have a wonderfully unique hostess gift or housewarming present.

Can't find a real fruit crate? Any small, shallow wooden box (or even corrugated cardboard) will do. Want to brighten your kitchen? Transform the drawer fronts into painted fruit labels like these!

PROJECT

1

These patterns may be hand-traced or photocopied for personal use only. Enlarge at 200% to bring them up to full size.

PAINT: DecoArt Americana

 Yellow Ochre
 Raw Sienna
 Salem Blue
 Milk Chocolate
 Buttermilk
 Jade Green

 Avocado
 Titanium White
 Berry Red
 Napa Red
 Black Green
 True Ochre

 Uniform Blue
 French Grey Blue
 Hauser Dark Green
 Navy Blue
 Soft Blue
 Country Red

 Dark Chocolate
 Light Avocado
 Black Plum
 Tomato Red
 Burnt Sienna

Yellow Ochre · Raw Sienna · Salem Blue · Milk Chocolate · Buttermilk · Jade Green · Avocado · Titanium White · Berry Red · Napa Red · Black Green · Cadmium Red · Uniform Blue · French Grey Blue · Hauser Dark Green · Navy Blue · Soft Blue · True Ochre · Dark Chocolate · Light Avocado · Black Plum · Tomato Red · Burnt Sienna · Country Red

Surface

- Wooden fruit crates

Brushes

- ¼-inch and ½-inch flats
- nos. 0 and 1 rounds
- nos. 10/0, 0 and 1 liners
- ½-inch rake brush
- small scruffy brush
- small mop or filbert

Additional Supplies

- Toothpicks
- Painter's tape
- Pennies
- Brush 'n Blend Extender
- DuraClear Satin Varnish

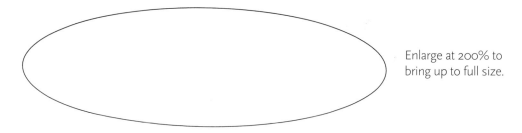

Enlarge at 200% to
bring up to full size.

Prepare Your Surface

The Raw Surfaces

1 Each of the three fruit designs begins the same way. Start by masking off the border area with one-inch painter's tape.

2 To create the concave corners, use pennies. Tape them down with the low-tack tape.

3 Basecoat with Yellow Ochre. Paint over the penny as you hold it down. Let this layer dry and paint another coat.

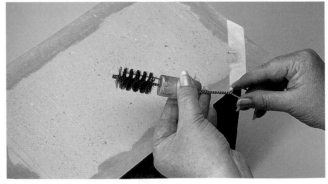

4 Using a spattering brush or toothbrush, spatter with thinned Milk Chocolate and Buttermilk. Thin the colors with water. Apply the oval template from the pattern on page 15.

The Sky, Clouds and Grass

5 Paint the top half of the oval with Salem Blue and let dry.

6 Stipple in the clouds with Titanium White on a scruffy brush. Soften the bottom of the clouds with a mop brush.

The Completed Clouds

7 Pat in the horizon with a scruffy brush loaded with Jade Green.

8 After you have pounced in the horizon line, sweep the brush across the oval with the Jade Green about halfway into the grass area. With the scruffy brush, sweep a mix of Avocado + Jade Green (1:1) and blend it into the lighter green to create the grass in the foreground.

9 Using a no. 1 liner brush loaded with Jade Green, outline the oval. Remove the tape and pennies after this has dried. Note: Don't worry about jagged edges. They'll be fixed by the border.

The Fruit

10 Paint the blueberries as instructed below. Using a no. 4 flat brush loaded with Uniform Blue, paint the outside border.

The Blueberries:

1. Use a ½-inch flat to base the leaves with Avocado and the berries with Uniform Blue. Base the small berries with French Grey Blue.
2. Shade the leaves with Hauser Dark Green. Outline the berries in Navy Blue and the small ones with Uniform Blue using a no. 1 round brush.
3. Pounce French Grey Blue in the large berries' center with a scruffy brush. With a ¼-inch flat, drybrush the leaves Jade Green and shade them with Black Green.
4. Highlight the berries with a dab of Soft Blue. Paint the blossom ends with Navy Blue using a no. 0 round. Highlight the blossom edges with a few strokes of Soft Blue.

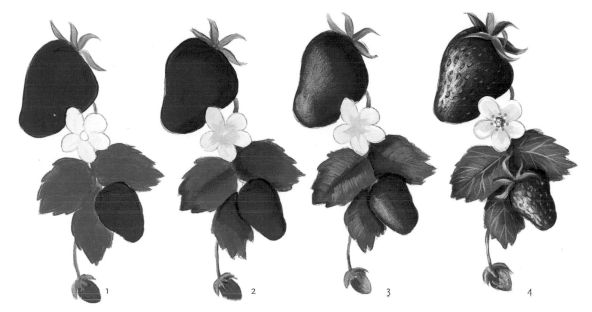

The Strawberries:

1. Base the berries with Berry Red using a ¼-inch flat. Base the leaves and stems with Avocado. Base the flower with Buttermilk.
2. Float Napa Red on the bottom right with a ¼-inch flat. Shade the leaves and stem with Black Green. Add a touch of Yellow Ochre to Buttermilk for the flower center and feather outward.

3. Mix Cadmium Red + Titanium White (1:1) and drybrush it on the berries with a ¼-inch flat. Apply only to the upper areas. Apply to the lower half of the unripe berry. Drybrush Jade Green on each leaf.
4. Use a no. 10/0 liner to paint the calyx, stems and veins on the leaves with Jade Green.

The Peaches:

1. Base the peach with True Ochre on a ¼-inch flat and the leaves with Avocado. Base the stem with Dark Chocolate on a no. 0 round.
2. Paint Brush 'n Blend over the dry True Ochre. Contour the peach with thinned Tomato Red on a no. 1 round. Soften the edges by blending toward the center. With the ½-inch rake brush, add more Tomato Red on the left side. Start the stroke at the base and blend upward and outward following the contour of the peach to add roundness. With a ¼-inch flat, float Black Green along the lower edges of the leaves and down the center of the lower leaf. Shade the underside of the curled leaf with a no. 0 round.

3. Using Tomato Red full strength, add more contour and blend inward, but don't cover your first contour strokes. Gradating the values of the color gives the illusion of roundness. Add a tiny bit of White to Dark Chocolate and use a no. 0 round to highlight the upper half of the stem. Dry brush Light Avocado onto each side of the leaf.
4. Float Black Plum onto the darkest edges of the peach and into the crease at the stem. Drybrush a hint of White onto the lightest parts of the leaf. Dilute Light Avocado and paint tiny veins on the underside of the curled leaf with a no. 0 liner. Drybrush White along the top edge of the stem with a no. 0 round.

11 Here's how the completed word "Blueberries" should look when you've finished painting all the letters. Follow the color instructions below for each letter. The colors for the words "Strawberries" and "Peaches" are shown at right.

Colors for the Blueberry Letters

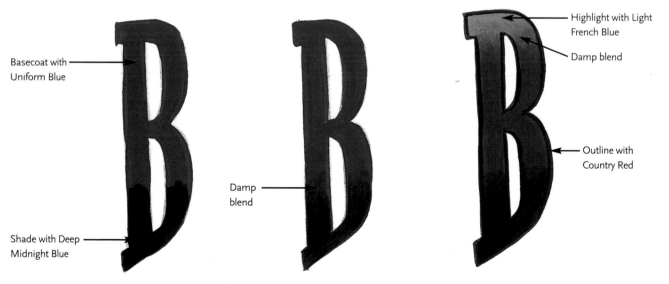

Basecoat with Uniform Blue

Shade with Deep Midnight Blue

Damp blend

Highlight with Light French Blue

Damp blend

Outline with Country Red

Colors for the Strawberry Letters

Basecoat
with Cadmium Red

Shade with Berry
Red

Damp
blend

Highlight with
Gooseberry
Pink

Damp blend

Outline with
Light Avocado

Colors for the Peach Letters

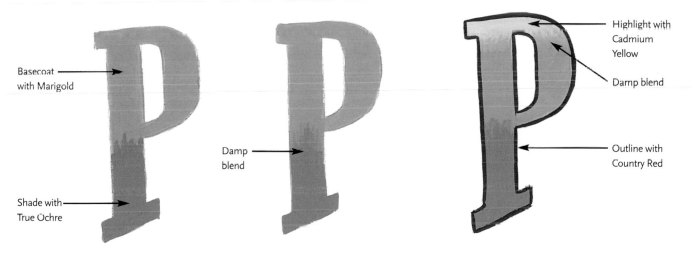

Basecoat
with Marigold

Shade with
True Ochre

Damp
blend

Highlight with
Cadmium
Yellow

Damp blend

Outline with
Country Red

12 Float around the inside edge of the border with Burnt Sienna side loaded on a ½-inch flat brush.

13 Outline the inner edge of the border with Salem Blue loaded on a no. 1 script liner.

14 Outline the blueberry letters with Country Red loaded on a no. 1 script liner. Outline the strawberry letters with Light Avocado and the peach letters with Country Red. (For details on painting the letters, see pages 20-21.)

15 Dilute Milk Chocolate with water and spatter lightly over the entire area with a spattering tool or toothbrush.

The Completed
Blueberry Crate

The Completed
Peach Crate

The Completed
Strawberry Crate

From Old Milk Can to
Fantastic
Farm Scene

Remember the "Early American" decorating craze in the 1970s? A big part of that look were those metal milk cans that were painted black with a gold eagle decal on the side. They were often placed on the front porch or used in the foyer to hold umbrellas.

Now, many of those old milk cans are ending up in flea markets and garage sales, just waiting to be recycled. And why not? They're easy to paint and fit right in with today's American and French country decorating themes.

They can still hold those umbrellas, or they can become a great planter. Or fit one with a small glass top and you have a unique side table.

PROJECT

Patterns for Farm Scene

These patterns may be
hand-traced or photocopied
for personal use only.
Enlarge at 200% to bring
up to full size.

PAINT: DecoArt Americana

| Americana Satins: Bright Blue | Americana Satins: White Satin | Salem Blue | Jade Green | Avocado | White Wash |

| Black Green | Soft Black | Slate Grey | Graphite | Dark Chocolate | Raw Sienna |

| Lamp Black | Country Red | Cadmium Red | Blue Grey Mist | Red Iron Oxide | Buttermilk |

| Yellow Ochre | Sapphire | Marigold | True Ochre | Burnt Sienna |

Surface

- Old milk can

Brushes

- 2-inch foam brush
- ½-inch and ¾-inch rakes
- nos. 5/0, 10/0, 0 and 1 liners
- nos. 1 and 10 rounds
- ¼-inch flat
- large mop brush
- 1-inch sponge
- medium scruffy brush

Additional Supplies

- Wire brush
- Primer
- Sea sponge
- Sanding sponge
- Americana Spray Sealer
- DecoArt Oak Gel Stain

Prepare the Milk Can

The Raw Surface

1 Scrape the flecks of paint off the milk can with a wire brush.

2 Prime the milk can with a primer such as Kilz and a large 2-inch foam brush.

The Sky, Clouds and Grass

3 Mix 2 parts Americana White Satin to 1 part Americana Bright Blue to make a pleasing sky color. Paint the top three-quarters of the milk can with this sky color using a 2-inch foam brush.

4 Pounce on a few clouds with a sea sponge loaded with Salem Blue.

5 Soften the clouds with a mop brush. Make circles and figure eights with a very light touch.

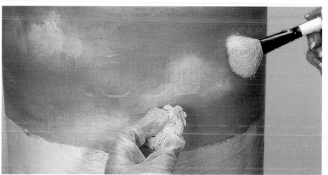

6 Apply White Wash in a smaller area over the previous clouds with a sea sponge. Soften with the mop brush and let dry.

7 Apply Jade Green at the horizon with the sea sponge. Soften into the sky with a mop brush. Sponge over this with Avocado, but do not soften.

8 The middle and foreground are created with Jade Green and Avocado, with the Avocado more toward the bottom of the milk can. Blend each color into the other with a mop brush.

The Tree

9 Apply the tree pattern. For the background foliage, pounce Black Green and Avocado using a scruffy brush.

10 Paint the tree trunk with White Wash loaded on a ¼-inch flat brush. Then add a touch of Lamp Black to the White Wash and paint the branches using a no. 1 script liner.

11 Paint more foliage on the top of the branches with Jade Green. Then highlight the foliage with a mix of Jade Green + White Wash (1:1).

12 Float diluted Soft Black on each side of the tree. Use the diluted Soft Black to paint cast shadows on the trunk.

The Completed Tree

Add more foliage as needed with the colors used previously. Add the trunk details with slightly diluted Soft Black. Dilute Burnt Sienna and randomly place the color on the trunk.

The Barn

14 Transfer the barn pattern onto the milk can. Undercoat the barn with White Wash.

15 Basecoat the barn with Country Red. For the shaded side of the barn, add a touch of Soft Black to the Country Red. Paint the inside of the barn with Soft Black.

16 With a ½-inch rake brush loaded with a mix of Country Red and Soft Black, add texture vertically to the front of the barn.

17 Add cracks in the boards with Soft Black. Float the shadow under the front eaves with Country Red and a touch of the black mix. On the shaded side, paint the shadow under the eaves with thinned Soft Black. Basecoat the roof with Blue Grey Mist.

The Barn

18 Drybrush a wash of thinned Dark Grey in the direction of the slant of the roof with a ½-inch rake. Using a no. 5/0 liner brush, paint the shadows on the roof where the tin overlaps.

The Completed Barn

Add the roof details with diluted Red Iron Oxide and Buttermilk using the rake brush. Add more shadow under the eaves if you need more contrast. Add a couple of lightning rods to the roof. Drybrush Soft Black sparingly in a few places on the barn wood. Then drybrush Cadmium Red up and down the sunny side of the barn. This will make it look warmer. Pounce a line of grass over the bottom edge of the barn and shade the grass to the right of the barn with Avocado and a bit of Black Green. With a medium scruffy brush, add a few bushes to anchor the barn.

The Pond and Checkerboard

20 Basecoat the pond with two coats of Salem Blue. Add Jade Green reflections with the ¾-inch rake brush by using a downward stroke.

21 Add Avocado to the edge of the water, and pull downward into the reflection with the rake brush. Use very thin Titanium White loaded on a no. 1 liner to paint the wispy swirls on the pond's surface. Apply very fine white lines on the far side of the pond where the water meets the ground. Above the line apply a very fine line of Black Green.

22 Add the grass to soften and obscure the back and edges of the pond. Using the no. 1 liner and different blends of Jade Green and Avocado, paint long blades of grass around the edge. Start at the bottom and pull straight up, ending your stroke with a taper. Apply some grass strokes so they appear to come out of the water.

23 Mix White Wash and just a touch of Soft Black to form a light gray. Paint two ovals overlapping the water's edge. Float Soft Black to shade them and drybrush White Wash on the top edges to highlight. Make the rocks appear to be submerged by painting a very fine white line of reflection where the water line should be.

24 Add the checkerboard by painting the bottom with Yellow Ochre and let dry. Using a 1-inch foam brush loaded with Country Red, paint the checkerboard pattern. The squares don't have to be exact.

The Morning Glories

25 Transfer the morning glory pattern to the milk can. It makes a nice design if you add the morning glories to the top and have them spilling over the side of the milk can.

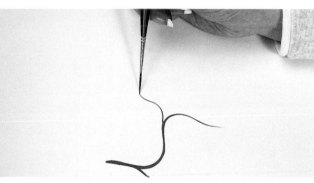

1 Paint the meandering vine with a no. 0 script liner loaded with thinned Avocado.

2 Using a ¾-inch flat brush loaded with Avocado, paint one half of the leaf. End on the chisel edge of the brush.

3 Turn your work to make painting more comfortable. Paint the second half of the leaf just like the first. Join the two halves at the leaf tip.

4 Add the stems with the no. 0 liner and thinned Avocado to finish.

Morning Glories Step by Step

✔ Load a no. 10 round brush with Sapphire.

✔ Push the brush so the bristles spread slightly, then turn the brush "just a hair."

✔ Pull the brush back and lift so the stroke ends in a slight point.

✔ Make more petals in the same manner, making sure they end toward the center or base of the first stroke.

✔ Turn your work and add the front petals, but do not end the strokes at a point.

✔ Use a ½-inch rake brush loaded with thinned White Wash to paint the center of the bloom by stroking outward. Do the same at the base of any unopened blooms. Paint the very centers with Marigold and shade with True Ochre.

The Windmill
and Daisy Bucket

26 A windmill in the distance is a nice country touch and it only takes a few strokes to complete.

27 No country scene is complete without the weathered fence post and old milking pail.

1

2

3

The Windmill

1. Transfer the windmill pattern onto the milk can. Basecoat the windmill with Burnt Sienna using a no.1 round brush.
2. Highlight the left side of the blades with a brush mix of Raw Sienna and a touch of White Wash.
3. Add the vane in the back with Dark Chocolate. Use a no.1 liner to paint the four legs and allow them to disappear into the distant foliage. Use Burnt Sienna to paint very fine cross wires on the legs.

The Rusty Pail

1. Basecoat outer pail Slate Grey with a ¼-inch flat brush. Mix a 1:1 ratio of Slate Grey and Graphite and paint the outer right side and the inside of the pail. Damp-blend the color to soften hard edges. Use the ¼-inch flat to add deeper shading of Graphite on the far right side of the pail, and the inner left side. Use a no.1 liner to stroke in stems of Avocado over Black Green.

2. Mix Slate Grey and Graphite (2:1) to make an "in-between" gray and apply down the middle of the outside and damp-blend into the light and dark side of the pail. Mix a very thin amount of White Wash and water, and dry-brush onto the outside of the pail, following the contour. Use a liner brush to add a lip around the top edge with Graphite. Use a no. 1 round to add shaded daisies (Slate Grey and White Wash 1:1), then more daisies on top of them in White Wash.

3. Use the no. 1 liner brush to add rings around the pail in Slate Grey and highlight with a thinned White Wash. Add the bale in Slate Grey, highlight with thinned White Wash and shade with Graphite. Thin Red Iron Oxide until watery and transparent and use a small round brush to add random patches of rust. Add daisy centers in Marigold and True Ochre and bring grass up over the front side of the pail to make it appear planted in the tall grass.

The Fence Post

1. Basecoat the post with Slate Grey using a ¼-inch flat. Let it disappear into the grass. Float White Wash along the left side of the post and shade with Graphite on the right.

2. With the same brush, drybrush White Wash on the post to give it a rough look. Use a no. 1 round loaded with Soft Black to create the deeper shadow (a thin line) on the right side.

3. Add cracks and knots to the wood with White Wash and Soft Black. Create barbed wire using a no. 10/0 liner loaded with Dark Chocolate, and highlight with Raw Sienna. With thinned Graphite, create the shadow of the wire on the post. Apply grass in varying shades of green in front of the post. Make the grass darker on the shady side and lighter on the sunny side.

1   2   3

From Chicken Trough to
Charming
Cottage

As soon as I saw this old metal watering trough for baby chicks, I remembered my Grandma had had them in her hen houses out on the farm. The dome-like cover lifts off to reveal the water well, and the water trickles into the shallow trough through hidden holes.

For baby chicks it had to sit on the ground, but I thought it would make a wonderful bird feeder or watering well for our backyard birds. In that case, it could hang from a branch or sit on a garden wall or tree stump.

These troughs are galvanized to be rustproof, and the plain smooth surface makes it a great painting project. This tudor cottage feeder will delight your backyard visitors—and the birds!

PROJECT

Pattern for Tudor Cottage

This pattern may be hand-traced or photocopied for personal use only. Enlarge at 143% to bring it up to full size.

PAINT: DecoArt Americana

Metal Paint: Sage Green	Metal Paint: Bright White	Milk Chocolate	Sand
Burnt Sienna	Dark Chocolate	French Grey Blue	White Wash
Raw Sienna	Slate Grey	Lamp Black	Graphite
Black Green	Avocado	Antique Rose	

Surface

- Metal watering trough for baby chicks

Brushes

- ¼-inch and no. 16 flats
- no. 3 round
- nos. 10/0, 0 and 1 liners
- ¾-inch filbert rake
- ¼-inch scruffy brush
- ¼-inch angle shader
- ½-inch deerfoot stippler

Additional Supplies

- Sea sponge
- DuraClear Satin Varnish

Prepare the Surface

The Raw Surface

1 Remove the bottom section. Prime it with Sage Green Metal Paint and the top with Bright White Metal Paint. Basecoat the middle with Sand and the top with Milk Chocolate.

2 Paint the thatched roof with a ¼-inch filbert rake using shades of Burnt Sienna and Sand. Drybrush on the different values. Add more Sand to lighten the mix as you go. Add accents of Dark Chocolate.

3 Basecoat the windows with French Grey Blue. Make a zigzag reflection with a no. 3 round brush loaded with thinned White Wash.

4 Make the leading on the window in a diamond shape with slightly thinned Dark Chocolate using a no. 0 liner brush.

The Windows,
Door and Trim

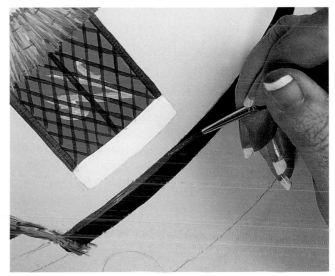

5 Paint the thatched overhang using a no. 0 liner brush with shades of Burnt Sienna, Sand and a bit of Dark Chocolate for accents.

6 Paint the trim with Dark Chocolate using a ¼-inch flat. Basecoat the windows with French Grey Blue. Make a zigzag reflection with a no. 3 round brush loaded with thinned White Wash. Highlight the trim with a no. 0 liner brush loaded with thinned Milk Chocolate.

7 Basecoat the front door with a mix of Raw Sienna + Dark Chocolate (1:1) using a no. 16 flat brush.

The Stone Foundation

8 Basecoat the rock foundation with Slate Grey. Create the individual stones with mixes of Graphite and Slate Grey, using a no. 3 round brush.

9 Randomly place these stones around the foundation.

 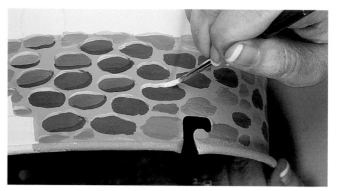

10 Shade the bottom of the stones with a no. 0 liner brush loaded with diluted mixes of Lamp Black + Graphite. Don't be too precise about the shadows. It will add character.

11 Highlight the stones with diluted White Wash using a no. 0 liner brush.

12 Show the separation in the boards of the door using a no. 10/0 liner brush loaded with thinned Lamp Black.

The Foliage

13 With a ¼-inch deerfoot stippler or a stiff bristle scruffy brush, shade the topiary with Black Green in the lower right corner of the circle. Do not clean the brush.

14 Pick up Avocado and pounce over the Black Green, just slightly blending the two colors. Do not clean the brush.

15 Mix White Wash +Avocado to make a light green. Pounce on the topiary in the upper left corner for a highlight.

16 Pounce the foliage into the window boxes the same way you did the topiary. For roses, add circles of Antique Rose over the dried foliage in the window boxes with a no. 1 liner brush. Do not clean the brush.

17 With the same liner brush, pick up White Wash on the tip. Highlight the roses with tiny comma strokes going in opposite directions.

The Finishing Touches

18 Float Milk Chocolate under the thatched roof with a ¼-inch angle shader, keeping the darker side of the brush next to the roof.

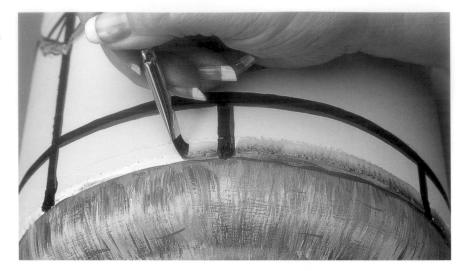

19 Shade both sides of the wood trim and windows with Milk Chocolate using the ¼-inch angle shader. Float shading around the right side of the top ball of the topiary. Around the bottom part of the topiary, shade with thinned Lamp Black.

20 Randomly pounce Avocado and White Wash on the bottom section of the chicken trough.

Detail of the Side

Add the vines on the thatched roof with a ½-inch scruffy brush or deerfoot stippler. Use the same greens as you did for the topiary on page 45.

The Completed Tudor Cottage

Apply DuraClear Satin Varnish before using your finished trough outside.

From Wash Tub to
a Garden of
Hydrangeas

What used to be a common sight in the backyard and on the farm is just as abundant at the flea markets today. All types of galvanized metal containers are scattered throughout, and that's why I wanted to bring home an old washtub and have some fun with it. They are usually priced to sell, so shop around for one that's in good condition.

I decided this washtub needed a bold design, yet be fast and easy to paint. Although these hydrangeas may look complicated, I promise this is an easy technique you will love to do again and again.

Paint one yourself and have a mini garden on the porch, patio or sunroom (add a matching watering can if you find one) — or fill your hydrangea washtub with pretty towels and set it beside your bathtub!

PROJECT

Pattern for Hydrangeas

This pattern may be hand-traced or photocopied for personal use only. Enlarge at 110% to bring it up to full size.

The Leaf Stamp

Materials

PAINT: DecoArt Americana

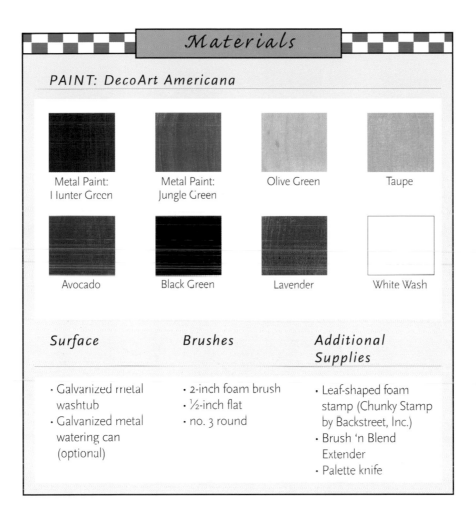

Metal Paint: Hunter Green	Metal Paint: Jungle Green	Olive Green	Taupe
Avocado	Black Green	Lavender	White Wash

Surface

- Galvanized metal washtub
- Galvanized metal watering can (optional)

Brushes

- 2-inch foam brush
- ½-inch flat
- no. 3 round

Additional Supplies

- Leaf-shaped foam stamp (Chunky Stamp by Backstreet, Inc.)
- Brush 'n Blend Extender
- Palette knife

Prepare the Surface

The Raw Surface: Watering Can

These can be picked up at a flea market or if you don't want to paint on an original can, you can get one at your local home and garden store.

The Raw Surface: Wash Tub

Again, you can get these at flea markets or garage sales, but if you don't want to paint on an antique, you can get a new one at your local home store.

1 Use a scrub brush and garden hose to wash off any dirt or debris and let dry. Paint about five inches inside the rim with Jungle Green Metal Paint. Using a 2-inch foam brush, paint the outside with Jungle Green and paint the bottom half with Hunter Green Metal Paint. Overlap the two colors in the middle; the overlap will be covered up later with large hydrangea blooms.

2 Pour a small amount of Hunter Green Metal Paint on a paper plate. Create a thin layer of paint by spreading the paint with a palette knife. Lay the foam leaf block in the paint and press lightly to ensure solid coverage. Randomly and loosely stamp leaves on the upper half of the tub on the light green background. Wash the leaf block with warm soapy water and pat dry. Pour Jungle Green Metal Paint on your palette and stamp leaves on the lower half of the tub, pointing the leaves downward.

The Hydrangea

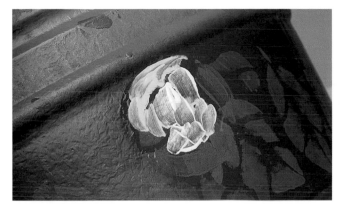

3 Brush on a very thin layer of Brush 'n Blend in a three-inch circle. On this wet glaze, dab small amounts of Olive Green, Taupe, Lavender and White Wash. Dab these colors on randomly, but don't add too much or it will run.

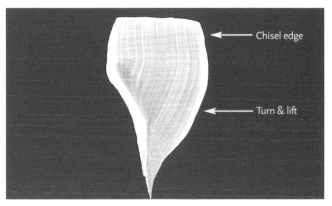

Chisel edge

Turn & lift

4 Paint the petals of the hydrangea with White Wash using a ½-inch flat brush. Start on the chisel edge, push down, turn and lift your brush back to the chisel edge.

5 Generously load a ½-inch flat with White Wash. On the outside of the circle, paint a straight comma stroke that points to the center of the bloom.

6 Don't rinse the brush, but do reload it with White Wash. Make a second petal in the same manner, opposite the first. The tails of the two strokes should meet.

7 Don't clean the brush. Finish the first flower with a fourth petal. Paint more flowers in the same manner right next to the first.

8 Continue painting flowers around the outer edge of the circle, reloading your brush with White Wash only when necessary.

9 Fill in the center of the hydrangea bloom with one or two more flowers. Continue painting blooms around the tub, keeping them toward the center so they can cover up the line where the two basecoats meet. Overlap the blooms and stagger them to keep it looking natural.

10 After all the blooms are painted and dried, load the ½-inch flat with White Wash and highlight each bloom with two or three flowers near the center. This layer of petals, which stays white and opaque, helps the other petals stay in the background, making the bloom look round.

11 Use a no. 3 round brush to dab three dots of Olive Green and/or Avocado in the center of the full flowers. Vary the color of the dots.

12 Add Black Green to Hunter Green and paint the filler leaves where you might need them to overlap the stamped leaves. Paint them right next to the blooms using a no. 3 round brush.

The Completed Washtub

The Completed Watering Can

From Kerosene Heater to
Cardinal In Winter

Here's an item you are bound to come across at a yard sale or flea market. Or maybe you already have and you've asked yourself, "What would I do with this?" Well, this idea is sure to warm you up.

After being fitted with an amber lightbulb, these old kerosene heaters make delightful conversation pieces and emit a golden glow that adds a warm ambience to the den or living room in the depths of winter.

You can find these heaters at the flea markets for around $12. Don't be concerned if it's not in working order because you will be removing the fuel tank if it is still intact. (This is a cinch—simply lift it out by its handle.)

Chances are the heater is going to be dirty, so spray it off with a garden hose when you get it home, and don't forget the inside where it's going to be very sooty. A long-handled scrub brush will help clean the inside.

This is a great painting project that is inexpensive and, adorned with a red velvet bow, makes a unique and welcome holiday gift.

PROJECT

5

Pattern for Cardinal
in Winter

This pattern may be hand-traced or
photocopied for personal use only.
Enlarge at 126% to bring it up to full
size.

Materials

PAINT: DecoArt Americana

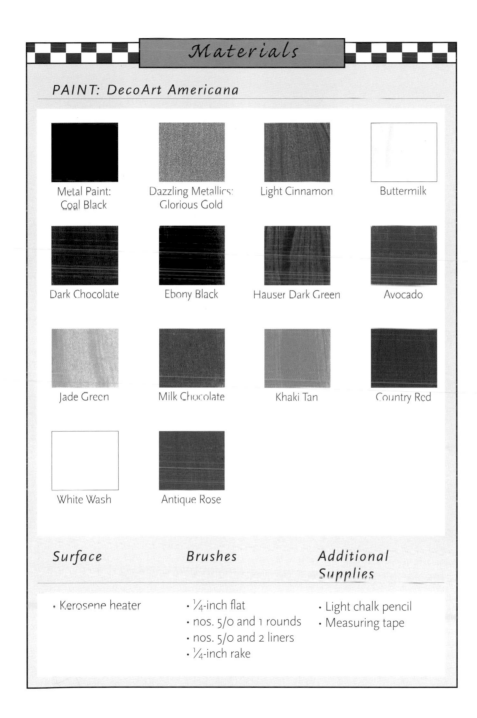

Metal Paint: Coal Black	Dazzling Metallics: Glorious Gold	Light Cinnamon	Buttermilk
Dark Chocolate	Ebony Black	Hauser Dark Green	Avocado
Jade Green	Milk Chocolate	Khaki Tan	Country Red
White Wash	Antique Rose		

Surface

- Kerosene heater

Brushes

- ¼-inch flat
- nos. 5/0 and 1 rounds
- nos. 5/0 and 2 liners
- ¼-inch rake

Additional Supplies

- Light chalk pencil
- Measuring tape

Prepare the Surface

The Raw Surface

1 Remove the old kerosene tank and discard. Then thoroughly scrub the heater inside and out and let dry before painting.

2 Cut a round piece of wood that will fit inside the kerosene heater. Mine was 9½ inches across. Drill a half-inch hole in the center for the light fixture, and another one about two inches away for the cord.

The Branches and Foliage

3 Basecoat the heater with Coal Black Metal Paint. Let it dry and apply the cardinal pattern with a light-colored chalk pencil.

4 Basecoat the branches with Light Cinnamon.

5 Highlight the branches by drybrushing Buttermilk using a ¼-inch flat.

6 Shade the branches with a float of Dark Chocolate using a ¼-inch flat. Add the deepest shading with a ¼-inch flat sideloaded with a mix of Dark Chocolate and a touch of Ebony Black.

7 Paint the evergreen needles with a no. 5/0 liner. The first layer is Hauser Dark Green, the second layer is Avocado and the third layer is Jade Green.

8 Basecoat the pine cones with Milk Chocolate. Reapply the pattern detail with a light colored pencil.

9 Paint the top edges of the cone scales with Khaki Tan using a no. 1 round. Where one scale overlaps another scale, shade slightly with Dark Chocolate.

The Cardinal

10 Undercoat the cardinal with White Wash. Red is a transparent color and will not cover the black. Undercoating will help the red to show up.

11 Basecoat the cardinal with two coats of Country Red. Mix Country Red + Milk Chocolate (1:1) and basecoat the beak and feet.

12 Add Avocado to Country Red to darken it just a little and shade the wing, tail, crest and neck. Add a small amount of Ebony Black to the beak color, and apply it around the eye. Add a small amount of White Wash to the Ebony Black for a dark gray and outline the eye using a no. 5/0 round.

13 Highlight the wings and tail with diluted Antique Rose using a ¼-inch rake brush. Apply individual feathers with the rake brush and a mix of Antique Rose + Country Red (1:1). Highlight the beak and feet with a mix of Antique Rose and a dot of White Wash.

14 Add the final shading and highlights to the feathers with Antique Rose. Mix one part Country Red with one part Avocado and a tad of Ebony Black and diluted White Wash. Shade the beak and feet further with this mix. Highlight the beak and eye with a dot of White Wash.

The Border

15 Add the decorative trim by marking off half-inch increments in six-inch long sections around the upper and lower edges of the base. Connect the marks diagonally to form a diamond-shaped grid. Draw two large parentheses on each end, facing in. These are your guides for comma strokes to come later.

16 Paint the lines with Glorious Gold using a no. 2 liner.

17 Connect the half-inch marks with small comma strokes. Close the diamond grids by painting large comma strokes where you drew the guides. In between the border sections, add a fleur-de-lis by making three comma strokes. Add three comma strokes on the feet, too. Paint all of these with Glorious Gold and the no. 2 liner.

The Finishing Touches

18 Install the light fixture in the wooden round per the instructions on the package. Place the wooden round and light fixture in the bottom of the heater where the tank used to be.

19 Screw in an amber light. Lightbulbs now come in many colors. You can use a red, yellow or white bulb. If you use a white bulb, I suggest you paint the inside walls of the heater with red or orange spray paint to give the heater an amber glow.

The Completed Heater

From Smoking Stand to
Nest Of
Chickens

It used to be that the man of the house was likely to have a smoking stand beside his favorite easy chair. It held pipes, tobacco and an ashtray. Because smoking has lost its social appeal, smoking stands have become obsolete and are not hard to find at flea markets. Their small size and unusual shapes make them a favorite surface of mine on which to paint.

PROJECT

Patterns for Nest of Chickens

These patterns may be hand-traced or photocopied for personal use only. Enlarge at 200% to bring up to full size.

PAINT: DecoArt Americana

 Americana Satins: Hunter Green

 Americana Satins: Tuscany Red

 Navy Blue

 Buttermilk

 Ebony Black

 Black Green

 Dark Chocolate

 Honey Brown

 Marigold

 Moon Yellow

 Dove Grey

 Sand

 Yellow Ochre

 Country Red

 Titanium White

 Warm Neutral

 Napa Red

 Avocado

 Terra Cotta

 Slate Grey

 Antique Rose

 Raw Sienna

 Asphaltum

 Hauser Dark Green

 White Wash

 Burnt Sienna

Surface

- Wooden smoking stand

Brushes

- ¼-inch dagger striper
- ¼-inch mop
- nos. 0 and 3 rounds
- ¼, ½, and 1-inch flats
- nos. 0 and 2 liners
- ¼ and ½-inch angle shaders

Additional Supplies

- Toothpicks
- 1-inch painter's tape
- DuraClear Satin Varnish
- DecoArt Oak Gel Stain

The Raw Surface

1 Basecoat the smoking stand with Americana Satins Hunter Green. Paint the trim with Americana Satins Tuscany Red. Paint the top with Buttermilk. Then transfer the hen pattern to one side of the stand.

The Hen and Rooster

2 Paint the grass blades with a ¼-inch dagger striper loaded first with Black Green. Use downward strokes for natural-looking grass. Using the same brush, add Avocado near the bottom of the piece. Highlight the grass by adding a touch of White Wash to the Avocado. Apply more Black Green where the hen's shadow will be cast on the ground.

3 Undercoat the hen and legs with Yellow Ochre. Undercoat the comb, crop and beak with White Wash.

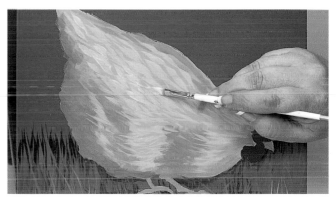

4 Shade the hen with a ¼-inch mop brush using mixes of Yellow Ochre, Terra Cotta and a bit of Slate Grey. Shade on the underside, around the thighs and under the neck. Create depth by shading the upper edge of the hen. Paint the beak and feet Marigold, and the comb and crop Country Red.

5 Mix Buttermilk and Yellow Ochre (1:1) Apply the first layer of feathers using a ¼-inch dagger striper, starting at the tail. Pull short strokes toward the hen's shoulder, overlapping the strokes. Press the brush so the wide side makes a carrot-shaped stroke. Make the strokes a bit thinner as you get closer to the neck. Do not paint feathers in the shading areas.

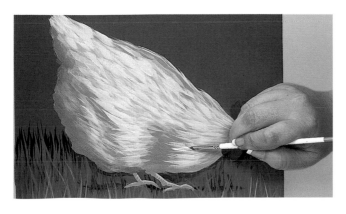

6 Apply the second layer of feathers in the same manner with diluted Buttermilk. Do not completely cover your first layer of feathers. Highlight the beak and feet with Buttermilk.

7 Apply the last layer of feathers with White Wash on top of the previous highlighting. Apply these feathers sparingly and with the thickest consistency of paint. Use a no. 3 round brush and Raw Sienna to paint texture on the feet. Create ripples and a scaly look with the tip of your brush.

8 Shade the comb and crop with Napa Red using a no. 3 round brush.

9 Highlight the comb and crop with Antique Rose on a no. 3 round brush. Damp blend to soften the edges.

10 Basecoat the eye with Raw Sienna. Float Raw Sienna around the edge of the comb and the bottom of the beak using a ¼-inch flat brush.

11 Paint the pupil with Ebony Black. Dip the end of your brush handle into the paint and make a dot in the center of the eye. Use a no. 0 round brush to paint a thin black line above the eyeball and the corner of the eye. After the pupil has dried, use a toothpick dipped into White Wash to create the light reflection in the eye at the edge of the pupil.

13 Paint the darker feathers on the underside of the rooster with the ¼-inch dagger striper and diluted Asphaltum. Make your strokes point toward the feet and then pull upward.

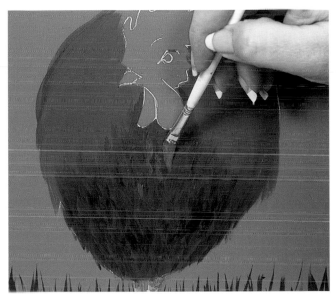

12 Transfer the pattern of the rooster to the other side of the smoking stand. Paint the grass as instructed on page 71. Basecoat the rooster's belly and chest with Dark Chocolate using a ½-inch flat brush. Paint the shoulders with Raw Sienna. Paint the feet as you did the hen's (see pages 71-72).

14 Mix Dark Chocolate and Raw Sienna (1:1) and dilute with water. Using the same brush, paint lighter feathers on the chest. This lighter color will bring the chest area forward, thereby creating depth.

15 Create the long mane feather shadows by diluting a mix of Ebony Black and Asphaltum (1:1). Apply long, jagged upward strokes using a no. 0 liner brush.

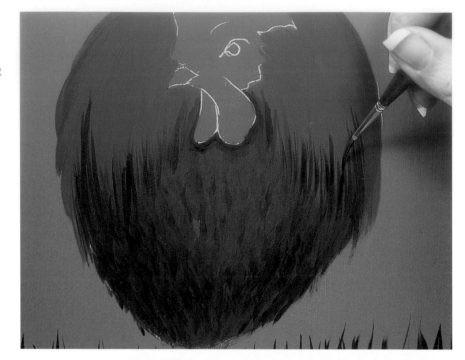

16 Paint the mane feathers with different values of Raw Sienna, Burnt Sienna and Sand. Dilute these colors so the paint flows smoothly from the brush. Make the top-most layer the lightest value.

17 Basecoat the first set of tail feathers with Hauser Dark Green. Shade down the sides and the centers of each feather with Black Green.

18 Paint the second set of tail feathers with Black Green.

19 Add detail to the tail feathers using a ¼-inch angle shader. Add a touch of White Wash to Hauser Dark Green. Drybrush the color on the edges of the feathers and near the centers. Slant your strokes upward as the feathers actually grow that way. On the darker feathers, mix Hauser Dark Green with Navy Blue to highlight. Then add a touch of White Wash to the mix and highlight the edges of the feathers.

20 Paint the head, eyes and beak as you did for the hen (see pages 71-72.) Float Dark Chocolate around the head to create the illusion that the head is in front of the body.

21 Mix a touch of Black Green and Hunter Green. Using a ½-inch flat brush, drybrush the background to the right of the rooster to create a shadow. Carry this color into the grass by painting blades of grass at the rooster's feet.

The Nest Box

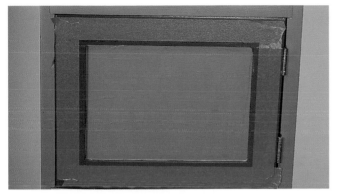

22 Using 1-inch painter's tape, mask off the inside edge of the door about ⅜-inch from the edge.

23 Paint the trim with Buttermilk and let dry.

24 With a ¼-inch flat brush loaded with Ebony Black, paint checks along the entire edge. Let this dry and remove the tape. Outline the checks with a no. 0 liner and Ebony Black.

25 Paint the background of the door with Black Green and let dry.

26 Basecoat the lower half of the door with Dark Chocolate and Ebony Black in randomly painted swaths with a 1-inch flat. This will help create depth and shadows. Use a no. 2 liner and Ebony Black to paint quick strokes of straw shaped shadows on what will be the back wall of the nest box.

27 Paint the first layer of straw by making bold Xs and random strokes with Honey Brown using the no. 2 liner brush. Make them extend to each side and up into the shadows previously painted, but do not cover the black completely.

28 Add another layer of straw using Marigold and the same liner brush. Be sure to allow some of the strokes to come out over the checkered border.

29 Add a few Moon Yellow highlights to some pieces of straw. Create shadows for the straw on the checkered border by diluting Ebony Black with water and painting a shadow to the bottom right of each piece of straw.

30 Once the straw is dry, transfer the egg pattern. Place the egg so it looks like it is in the straw. Undercoat the egg with Dove Grey. Basecoat the egg with Sand.

31 Dilute Yellow Ochre with water and float it around the edge of the egg with a ½-inch angle shader.

32 When the first shading is dry, dilute Dark Chocolate with water and float it around the bottom and ends of the egg. Highlight the egg in the fattest part with White Wash. Damp blend the white to soften the hard edges.

33 With Honey Brown and then Marigold, paint a few blades of straw across the lower front of the egg. This will "nestle" the egg in the straw and prevent the egg from appearing to float.

The Gingham Plaid

34 Apply two strips of 1-inch painter's tape parallel to each other and one inch apart. To space evenly, lay down three strips side by side. Remove the middle strip and place it next to the third on the opposite side, and place a new strip next to it. Again remove the spacer. This will guarantee perfect stripes.

1	
2	SPACER
3	
SPACER	
4	

How to lay down the tape to create straight rows.

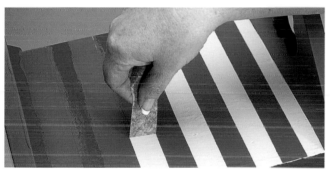

35 Paint the stripes a mix of Country Red + Warm Neutral (1:1). Let this dry, but remove the tape when the paint is still soft. Always pull the tape away at a 90° angle.

36 Allow the stripes to dry, ideally for several hours. Lay a second row of tape perpendicular to the first. Be sure to mask off other areas, like the sides.

37 Paint these stripes Country Red. Let dry, but again, remove the tape when the paint is still soft.

Where the stripes intersect and overlap, paint each square with Napa Red using a ¼-inch flat brush.

38 Using a no. 2 liner brush loaded with Avocado, pull the meandering vine and a few stems. Double load a no. 16 flat brush with Black Green and Avocado. Place the Avocado corner of the brush on the base of the stem and angle the chisel at a 45° angle. Press the brush down and pull the stroke, slightly wiggling the brush to make the scalloped edge. End the stroke back up on the chisel edge, creating the tip of the leaf.

39 Do the exact same stroke to create the other half of the leaf. Turn your surface to make painting more comfortable. Make sure the centers butt up against each other.

40 Create a diverse look in the leaves by painting a few side views. Do this with the same double-loaded brush, but make your stroke a bit more shallow and curve it slightly. Make sure the Black Green corner of the brush is the side you start with at the stem.

41 Add more stems and leaves as you desire. Make your leaves varied by turning the brush and changing the color sides. For instance, have darker leaf centers and lighter edges, or have lighter leaf centers and darker edges. Use the no. 0 liner to paint the center vein down each leaf in Avocado. Use a ¼-inch flat brush to drybrush a mix of Avocado + White Wash and highlight the leaves between the center and the edges.

42 Use a ¼-inch mop brush loaded with Marigold to make the black-eyed Susan petals using a press and pull stroke. Make the top petals short. Pull the stroke toward the center of the flower.

43 Continue making the petals around the flower. Turn your work to make painting more comfortable. Make the petals on the front of the flower a bit longer.

44 Use the same filbert brush to paint a few buds with Marigold. Make the stroke come to a point. Create a calyx with both Avocado and Black Green loaded on a no. 3 round brush. Paint an oval of Burnt Sienna in the center of the open flower. Make dip-dots of Burnt Sienna around the oval, but not touching it. Let this dry. Lighten the left side of the center with a bit of White Wash and Burnt Sienna. Shade the right side with Dark Chocolate applied in a crescent shape. Damp blend to soften hard lines. Make a final highlight on the center by adding a few dip-dots of Sand on the left side.

The Final Touches

Detail of the Completed Rooster

Detail of the Completed Hen

The Completed Smoking Stand

Finish the project by applying Dura-Clear Satin Finish over the acrylic artwork and antiquing the entire piece with Oak Gel Stain following the directions on the label.

From Broken Table to
Faux Delft Tiles

I have always enjoyed collecting Delft tiles from Holland. I love the vivid cobalt color and the simplicity of the art. When I visited a shop in Holland, Michigan, I became hooked all over again. They produced everything in Delft blue—pottery, dinnerware, jewelry, even cuckoo clocks. That visit inspired me to paint my own faux Delft tiles, but to do it on this unusual little table. The bottom shelf has a 4-tile design, and even the legs are decorated. It's so easy to paint, you'll want to accessorize a whole room!

PROJECT

Patterns for Faux Delft Tiles

These patterns may be hand-traced or photocopied for personal use only. Enlarge at 154% to bring up to full size.

PAINT: *DecoArt Americana*

Americana Satins:
White Satin

Prussian Blue

Red Violet

Titanium White

Ice Blue

Graphite

Dazzling Metallics:
Glorious Gold

Delft Blue Dark:
Mix 2 parts Prussian
Blue + 1 part Red
Violet + a touch of Ti-
tanium White to take
the "blackness" out.

Delft Blue Medium:
Mix 1 part Delft
Blue Dark + 3 parts
Delft Blue Light.
Thin with water to
make translucent.

Delft Blue Light:
Mix 1 part Delft Blue
Dark + 6 parts Tita-
nium White

Surface

- Old wooden table
  found at flea market

Brushes

- 2-inch foam brush
- 1-inch bristle brush
- ¼-inch and 1-inch
  flats
- nos. 1 and 10 rounds
- ½-inch scruffy
- no. 0 liner

Additional Supplies

- Primer (such as Kilz
  or BIN)
- 24-inch straightedge
- Pencil
- Painter's tape
- Valspar Porcelain
  Crackle Medium
- DecoArt Gel Stain
- DecoArt Faux Glazing
  Medium
- Soft cloth
- DuraClear Satin
  Varnish

Prepare the Surface

1 When I found this table, I really liked the charm of the turned spindle legs but part of the top had been broken. This didn't deter me, nor should it deter you if the price is right. I removed the broken top and lightly sanded the legs. Then I primed them using two coats of a good stain-hiding primer.

2 Buy a piece of good wood from your local home improvement center that measures about 18" x 24" x ¾". I had my husband cut the wood to 18" x 18" square.

CAUTION: THIS STEP REQUIRES THE USE OF A TABLE SAW AND ROUTER. DO NOT ATTEMPT TO CUT THE WOOD YOURSELF UNLESS YOU ARE EXPERIENCED WITH THE APPROPRIATE POWER TOOLS. YOUR LOCAL HOME IMPROVEMENT CENTER CAN CUT THE WOOD FOR A NOMINAL FEE.

Don't attach the new top to the legs just yet. It is easier to paint the top when it isn't attached. Paint the legs and top with Americana Satins White Satin. Use a 2-inch foam brush for the tabletop and a 1-inch bristle brush for the turned legs. The legs of your table will most likely be different than what I have here, so use your imagination to embellish them with flowers and comma strokes.

Paint the Tabletop

3 Using a two-foot straightedge, measure 3½ inches in to create a border and a ten-inch square in the center of the tabletop. If your table top has a routered edge, measure in from the inner edge.

4 Transfer the windmill scene pattern to the tabletop. You'll be painting the entire scene first, then dividing it into four "tiles."

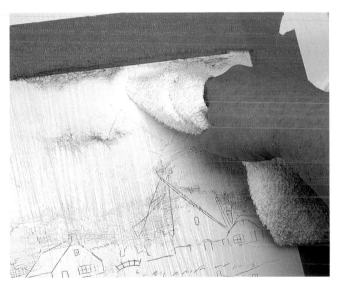

5 This design is painted with three different values of one base color—Delft Blue Dark. See color chart on page 87 for mixing ratio. Mask off the ten-inch square with low-tack tape. Be sure to burnish the edges. Mix three parts Delft Blue Dark with ten parts Faux Glazing Medium. Brush this glaze mix over the top part of the design. Using a towel or soft cloth, wipe out part of the glaze mix to indicate clouds. The glaze will take off some of the pattern, so reapply it if necessary.

6 Using Delft Blue Light as your first layer of color, apply with a ¼-inch flat and a ½-inch scruffy brush for the trees. Your brushstrokes should show and look muddy.

7 Apply Delft Blue Medium to add shading and more detail. Again, use the ¼-inch flat and the scruffy brush. The lines are added with a no. 0 liner.

8 Use a no. 0 liner brush loaded with Delft Blue Dark to sparingly add outlines around objects and to deepen shadows.

9 Once the last step is dry, carefully peel off the tape.

OOPS! If this happens to you...

Did you burnish your tape really well, but the paint still bled under the tape? Don't despair!

Fix the bleed with a little Faux Glazing Medium on a soft cloth or Q-tip. Lightly rub where the paint came under the tape. Be careful not to go onto the picture. This works if you have put some unwanted paint on your piece as well.

The Individual Tiles

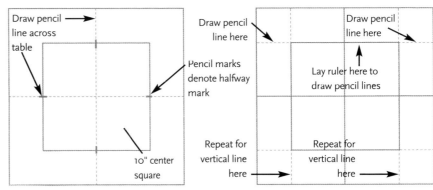

10 Lightly mark off the halfway point of the center square (at five inches) on each side of the square. Line up your marks with a straight edge and draw a light horizontal line from one side to the other. Do the same vertically.

Line up the straightedge along each side of the center square and draw a line from the corners of the center square to the edge of the table. Do this on all sides.

11 With Delft Blue Light loaded on a ¼-inch flat brush, make the flowers in the corner.

12 Using Delft Blue Medium loaded on the no. 0 liner brush, add the shading to the flowers.

13 With Delft Blue Dark loaded on the no. 0 liner, outline the flower and add curlicues and dots.

14 Use a no. 1 round brush to make the little comma strokes in the four corners of the other tiles. Use both the Delft Blue Light and Medium colors for this step.

Create Grout Lines

15 Create the "grout" between the tiles using a no. 0 liner loaded with Ice Blue. Paint only the lines running horizontally, so you don't smear the lines.

16 Repeat Step 15 for the vertical grout lines. Where the grout crosses the darker portions of the painting, you'll need to go over the area twice. Let it dry between applications.

17 Mix Ice Blue + Graphite (1:1) and thin it with water. Shade the grout with a no. 1 liner brush. Make sure this mixture is very thin.

Highlight the grout on the opposite side of the shading with a no. 1 liner brush loaded with Titanium White. Paint the highlight on all four sides of the inside tiles, but on the blue areas only. Thin the white as little as possible.

Age the Tiles

18 Apply the crackle medium with a foam brush. Try not to get it too thick. Let this dry as instructed on the bottle. Don't forget to apply the crackle medium to the lower shelf, if there is one, but not to the legs or undersides.

19 Some crackle mediums are designed to crack the paint underneath. Notice the tiny porcelain-like cracks on this piece.

20 Mix Ice Blue + Gel Stain (1:3). Brush this mixture on one tile at a time with a 1-inch flat brush. Slip-slap it on. You should brush this mixture over the rest of the piece as well to keep the piece consistent.

21 Be sure to wipe the gel stain mixture off quickly. The stain will stay in the cracks.

Add Trim and
Attach Table Top

22 Add the gold trim on the table with a no. 10 round brush loaded with Glorious Gold.

23 Measure the halfway point on each side of the table-top and halfway on each side of the table base. Now line up the marks.

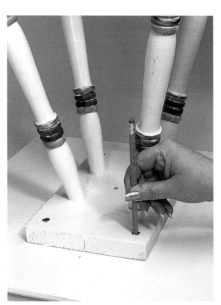

24 Mark the screw holes with your pencil.

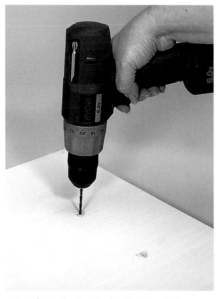

25 Drill pilot holes in the table top for the screws. Don't make them too deep or you'll risk going right through your painting. Realign the base and tabletop.

26 Use a screwdriver or a drill with a screw bit to tighten the screws, securing your tabletop to the base. Make sure you have the correct length of screw or the screw will come through your painting.

Details of the Completed Project

Detail of the Lower Shelf

Detail of the Table Legs

Detail of the Table Top

The Completed Table

Apply a coat of DuraClear Satin Varnish to areas of the legs that were painted with acrylic paint. Don't apply it to the crackled areas.

Faux Delft Clock

This is one of my favorite designs to paint. It's cheery and a classic, and lends itself well to many paintable surfaces. I'm always adapting the design to the project at hand, so feel free to add your own little touches as well. And you don't have to go to the flea market to find something to paint. Just look at how great the Delft design looks on this clock, which is from Walnut Hollow and is available through many craft stores.

From Lingerie Chest to
Pretty Hollyhock Heaven

This four-drawer chest would make a pretty addition to any bedroom or bath. Creamy white hollyhocks are set against lush green foliage in a monochromatic design.

When I found this chest at the flea market, it looked so sad but showed a lot of promise. It needed an all-over design that would camouflage the imperfect surface, and I thought these hollyhocks would do just that.

The chest had been in a shed, so the first thing I did was take out all the drawers and vacuum inside them and all around the outside of the chest to remove dirt and cobwebs. When it was clean inside and out, I removed the drawer knobs to make it easier to sand and prepare the chest for painting.

PROJECT

Patterns for the Hollyhocks

This pattern may be hand-traced or photocopied for personal use only. Enlarge at 110% to bring it up to size.

This pattern may be hand-traced or photocopied for personal use only. Reduce at 80% to bring it down to size.

PAINT: DecoArt Americana

Americana Satins: Soft White

Americana Satins: Sage Green

Very light white/green mix

Hauser Dark Green

Black Forest Green

Forest Green

Jade Green

Black Green

Light Buttermilk

Dove Grey

Titanium White

True Ochre

Surface

- Wooden 4-drawer chest

Brushes

- 2-inch foam brush
- nos. 1 and 2 rounds
- nos. 10/0 and 2 liners
- ¼-inch and ½-inch flats

Additional Supplies

- Primer
- Sea sponge
- Toothpick
- Wood replacement knobs (optional)
- Yard stick or long ruler
- Dark Chocolate acrylic paint (optional)
- Palette knife (optional)
- DuraClear Satin Varnish

Make Any Needed Repairs

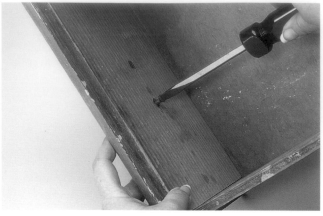

1 Remove all of the hardware and old drawer pulls. I recommend replacing the pulls with inexpensive wooden knobs from your local home improvement center.

2 If the old pulls have been painted over, using a hammer to lightly tap them may help remove them. Be sure to remove the screws first.

3 If a drawer is wobbling, shore it up with a few nails on the bottom back of the drawer.

4 A little wood glue will reinforce worn joints.

5 Tap in any original nails that might be sticking out.

6 Fill in the original nail holes with wood putty.

Prepare the Surface

7 Prepare the piece by sanding the chest and drawers really well and removing the sanding dust with a tack cloth. Prime all the outside surfaces with a good stain-hiding primer. Let this dry at least twenty-four hours.

Basecoat the surface with a mix of Americana Satins Soft White + Americana Satins Sage Green (8:1) using a 2-inch foam brush. The mix should be white with the slightest hint of green. Paint the chest and the drawer fronts with two coats if you need to. Paint the replacement knobs the same color. When the drawers and knobs are completely dry, attach the knobs with screws and place the drawers back in the chest. The knobs will be blended into your design.

Mix Hauser Dark Green and the white/green basecoat (1:1) and sponge this on the bottom front of the chest, going about halfway up. Gradually sponge lighter and more sparingly so that the color tapers off as it goes higher on the chest.

The Background
and Leaves

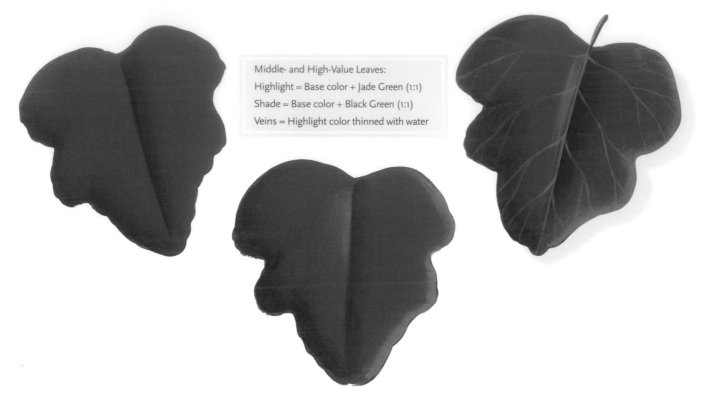

Middle- and High-Value Leaves:
Highlight = Base color + Jade Green (1:1)
Shade = Base color + Black Green (1:1)
Veins = Highlight color thinned with water

8 Since there are so many leaves and they cover a lot of surface, I've made them as simple as possible.

✓ Draw two or three stalks vertically on each side of the cabinet and the front. You may need to put more on your cabinet if it's wider. Do this by holding a yard stick against the surface and drawing a line from the tip of the stem down. It doesn't matter where the stalk ends because it will disappear into the foliage. The tips of the stems should be staggered to look more natural. Paint the stalk Black Forest Green with a no. 2 liner brush.

✓ There are three basic leaf shades used here, and you should start with the darkest since they are obscured by the others that overlap them. Sketch these first leaves around the stems. Don't worry about perfection here. No leaf should be shaped just like the others, so draw them freely but sparingly. If you don't trust yourself enough to draw the leaves, use the pattern on page 100. Keep in mind that the leaves get smaller as they go up the stem. Stop the leaves about three-quarters of the way up the stalk. Use a ½-inch flat brush loaded with Black Forest Green to paint all the base leaves and let dry.

✓ Draw more leaves on the stems, overlapping the darker leaves in most places, but not completely covering them. Again, make them smaller as you go up the stem. Paint the middle value leaves with Forest Green. When these dry, apply the highlights, shading and veins according to the illustration above.

✓ Mix Forest Green and Jade Green (1:1) for the last layer of leaves. These leaves overlap all of the other leaves. Make plenty of them and fill in any gaps you think should be filled with foliage. The idea is to make the clusters of hollyhocks look thick and lush, so there should be no background showing through at the base of the plants. Most of the stems should be obscured by now. Highlight and shade these leaves as directed in the illustration above.

The Hollyhocks

9 The big, creamy hollyhock blooms wind their way up and around the center stalk, getting smaller as they go.

✓ Add buds to the top of the stems using Black Forest Green loaded on a no. 2 round brush. Mix Black Green and Black Forest Green (1:1) and apply shading on the right side of the stem and buds. Highlight the buds with a few strokes of Jade Green. Run a thin line of Jade Green down the left side of the stem with a no. 2 liner.

✓ Draw the outlines of the hollyhock blooms with a pencil; refer to the pattern for placement. Base the blooms with Light Buttermilk using a ¼-inch flat brush. Where a bloom overlaps a dark leaf, undercoat the bloom with Dove Grey, then base as directed above.

✓ Replace the pattern and transfer the inside lines of the flower. Paint Jade Green around the center of the flower with a ¼-inch flat brush and damp-blend outward to soften any hard edges. Apply Titanium White as a highlight on the outer edges of the petals. Use a ¼-inch flat and damp blend inward.

✓ Paint the outlines of the petals with Jade Green loaded on a no. 10/0 liner.

✓ Paint lines of Jade Green veins coming outward from the center of the each petal. Use the no. 10/0 liner and very thin paint, and slightly shake your hand to create a more natural vein.

✓ Paint the center with True Ochre using a no. 1 round brush.

✓ Mix Titanium White and True Ochre (1:1) and make about nine dots in the flower centers using a toothpick. When these are dry, highlight a few on the left side with a toothpick and Titanium White.

✓ Apply a bit more shading around the center by mixing a touch of Black Forest Green into Jade Green. Apply it to the right of the center and where the petals overlap one another.

✓ On buds and semi-open blooms, use the same highlighting and shading techniques. Apply the calyx and stems after the blooms are painted. Shade and highlight them as you did the closed buds.

Put the "Wear and Tear" on the Dresser

10 If you would like to give your hollyhock chest an aged look, you can add some faux "wear and tear" without interfering with the painting. Pick up Dark Chocolate acrylic paint on the back of a palette knife. Make sure the paint is thin on the back of the knife. A large amount of paint will make blobs on the surface. If you do get a blob on the surface, immediately wipe it off with a damp towel.

11 Apply a little bit of paint by running the back of the knife along the edges where there would naturally be wear and tear. Apply it like you would butter to a piece of bread.

12 Skip over some areas to give it a more natural appearance. Corners usually get the most abuse, so that's where you would add more of the Dark Chocolate.

Detail of the side of the dresser.
If you wish, continue the hollyhock design around both sides of the chest, varying the size and placement of the blossoms and leaves.

The Completed Chest

From Old Picnic Basket to
Beautiful Bonny-Blu

I love old labels and signs with their rich colors and ornate lettering. They were the perfect inspiration for this design. I bought this old picnic basket at the flea market featured in the front of this book. Its lid was just the right size and shape for my Bonny-Blu design. The design also lends itself well to other surfaces like a wooden tray. Paint it on your own basket and get lots of "wow's" at your next picnic!

9

PROJECT

Patterns for
Bonny-Blu Basket

These patterns may be hand-traced
or photocopied for personal use only.
Enlarge at 180% to bring up to full size.

BONNY-BLU® BAKING CO.

©KERRY TROUT

Materials

PAINT: DecoArt Americana

 Yellow Ochre

 True Ochre

 Titanium White

 Ice Blue

 French Grey Blue

 Medium Flesh

 DeLane's Dark Flesh

 Antique Rose

 Soft Peach

 Light Cinnamon

 Wedgewood Blue

 Shading Flesh

 Soft Black

 Charcoal Gray

 Dark Chocolate

 Deep Midnight Blue

 Slate Grey

 Raw Umber

 Raw Sienna

 Honey Brown

 Avocado

Surface

- Wooden picnic basket found at flea market

Brushes

- no. 2 mop
- ¼-inch, ½-inch and 1-inch flats
- no. 8 flat
- nos. 0 and 1 liners
- nos. 1 and 3 rounds
- ¼-inch and ¾-inch rakes

Additional Supplies

- Weathered Wood Crackle Medium
- Sea sponge
- Brush 'n Blend Extender
- no. 2 pencil
- Sanding sponge
- DecoArt Oak Gel Stain
- Ivory eyelet lace (optional)
- DecoArt Acrylic Spray Sealer (Satin)

The Raw Basket

1 Basecoat the top with Yellow Ochre and let dry. Apply Weathered Wood Crackle Medium in a thin layer according to the directions and let dry.

2 With a damp sea sponge, pounce True Ochre over the Weathered Wood Crackle. Try not to go over the same area twice as the paint will lift from the surface. Let dry completely.

3 Using the same sea sponge, pounce again with a mix of True Ochre and Yellow Ochre (1:2). Let dry.

4 Apply Titanium White to the previous mix. Pounce this color in the center of the basket lid with the sea sponge and soften it with a no. 2 mop brush.

The Hat and Face

5 Apply the pattern, but not the lettering. That will be done last. Basecoat the bonnet with Ice Blue. Near the head, float French Grey Blue using a 1-inch flat brush.

6 Blend Brush 'n Blend Extender and Titanium White into the bonnet in the lighter area. Outline the rim with a no. 1 liner brush loaded with Titanium White. Blend more if necessary for a nice gradation of color.

7 Base in the face with a no. 8 flat brush loaded with Medium Flesh. Allow the pattern marks to show through. This will make it easier to paint the shadows and highlights. You'll need to apply two coats of this base color, but maintain the lines of the eyes and nose.

8 Float around the perimeter of the eyes, nose and face with DeLane's Dark Flesh and blend it into the base color. Feel free to use the Brush 'n Blend to make the blending easier. Use the Brush 'n Blend and Antique Rose on the cheeks to give them a glow. Blend into the base color.

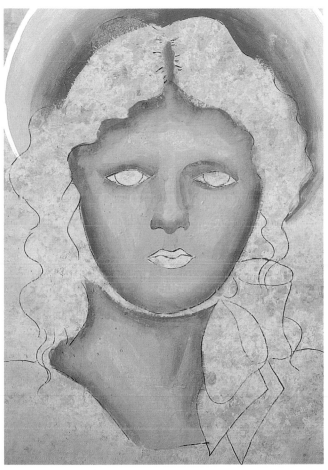

9 Highlight the forehead, nose, cheeks, chin, neck and eyebrow areas with Soft Peach and Brush 'n Blend Extender. These are the parts of the face that would be closest to the viewer.

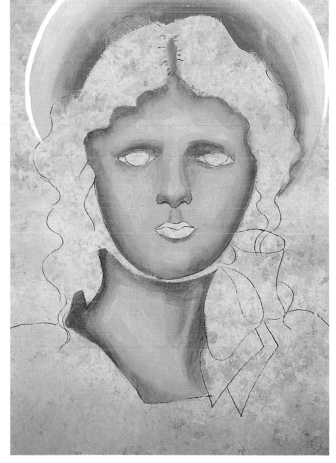

10 Deepen the shading with a mix of DeLane's Dark Flesh + Light Cinnamon (1:1). Thin this mix with water or the blending medium. Apply this thin mix with a no. 1 round brush around the bottom of the nose.

The Eyes

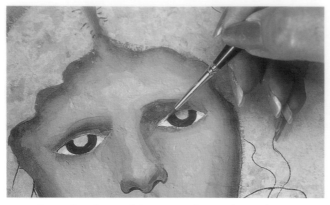

11 Paint the whites of the eyes with Ice Blue and Titanium White using a no. 1 round brush. Paint the iris with Wedgewood Blue using a no. 1 round brush. Using Ice Blue, apply the shadow of the eyelid with a no. 1 round brush.

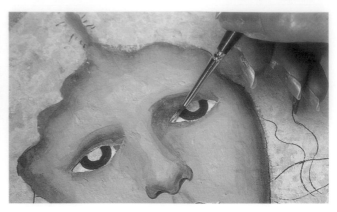

12 Mix Antique Rose + Shading Flesh (1:1). Make a triangular shape in the inner corner of each eye.

13 Highlight the iris with a mix of French Grey Blue and Wedgewood Blue. Allow some of the basecolor to show around the edges. Add a little Titanium White to the above mix and apply the final highlight in a smaller area.

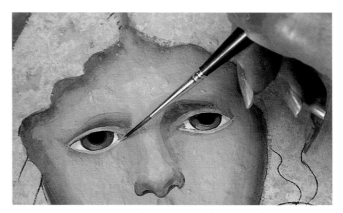

14 Paint the pupil with two coats of Soft Black. Highlight the eyelids (upper and lower) with Medium Flesh and a touch of Soft Peach using a no. 1 round brush.

15 Make the eyelid crease with a mix of Light Cinnamon and Charcoal Grey using a no. 1 liner brush.

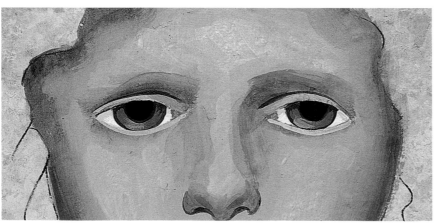

16 Apply the second highlight to the eyelids with Soft Peach and a touch of Titanium White using a no. 1 round brush.

17 Apply the upper eyelashes with a no. 0 liner brush loaded with a mix of Soft Black + Light Cinnamon (1:2). Apply the lower lashes with Light Cinnamon only.

18 Lightly sketch on the eyebrows with a no. 2 pencil.

19 Paint the eyebrows with a no. 0 liner brush loaded with Light Cinnamon. Make very fine, short strokes.

20 Apply the reflective light at the eight o'clock position at the edge of the pupil with a no. 0 liner brush loaded with Titanium White.

The Lips

21 Base the lips with Shading Flesh using a no. 1 round brush. Cover the outer lines, but leave the middle line as a reference.

22 Shade the lips with a thin glaze of Antique Rose. Contour the lips with DeLane's Dark Flesh, but don't make the lines harsh. You don't want to outline the lips.

23 In the corners of the mouth, apply Dark Chocolate. Highlight the lips with a mix of Shading Flesh + Soft Peach (1:2) using the no. 0 liner brush. Add a soft dot of Soft Peach for a final highlight using the no. 0 liner brush.

24 Add the final highlights to the skin with a mix of Titanium White + Soft Peach (1:1). Highlight the end of the nostrils and damp blend into the base colors. Highlight under each nostril and damp blend. Add a little Brush 'n Blend to your brush. Apply a thin line of the highlight color down the bridge of the nose and damp blend. Apply a stronger highlight of Titanium White to the chin and tip of the nose.

The Dress and Bow

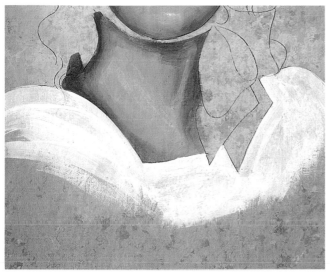

25 Base in the dress using a ½-inch flat brush loaded with Titanium White. Use very loose strokes.

26 Apply the shading with the ½-inch flat brush loaded with Titanium White and a touch of Wedgewood blue. Create the stripes with the ½-inch flat brush loaded with very thin Wedgewood Blue.

27 Basecoat the ribbon with Wedgewood Blue.

28 Shade the bow with Deep Midnight Blue using a ¼-inch flat.

29 Mix one part Slate Grey to three parts Wedgewood Blue. Apply the first highlighting.

30 Add a touch of Titanium White on the brush for the second highlighting. Do not go beyond the previous highlight area.

31 Apply the final highlight using a no. 1 liner brush with Titanium White and a little Brush 'n Blend. Apply this highlight in a smaller area than the previous highlights.

The Hair

32 Basecoat the hair with Raw Umber. You'll need to apply two coats. Apply the first highlight with Light Cinnamon in a slightly smaller area, then basecoat using a ¼-inch flat and a no. 1 liner for the contours and individual hairs.

33 Apply the second highlight with Raw Sienna using a ¼-inch flat brush and a no. 1 liner for the contours.

34 Apply the third highlight with Honey Brown using a ¾-inch filbert rake brush.

35 Apply the fourth highlight with Yellow Ochre using a ¼-inch filbert rake brush. Sparingly use a mix of Titanium White and Yellow Ochre loaded on a no. 1 liner brush to add the final highlights.

The Lettering

36 Base the letters with a thin wash of Raw Sienna, one coat only, using a ¼-inch flat brush.

37 With a ¼-inch flat brush loaded with Light Cinnamon and Brush 'n Blend, blend down on the "Bonny-Blu" letters and up on the "Baking Co." letters.

38 Outline all of the letters with Dark Chocolate and a no. 1 liner brush.

The Wheat Sprig

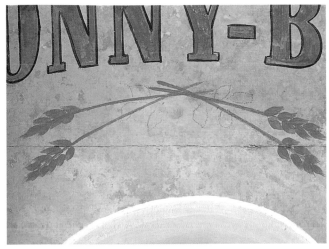

39 Using a no. 1 liner brush, paint the wheat stems with Honey Brown. With a no. 3 round brush, paint the husks.

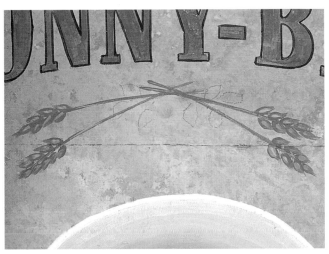

40 Add Titanium White to the Honey Brown (1:1) and paint the highlights on the stems and husks.

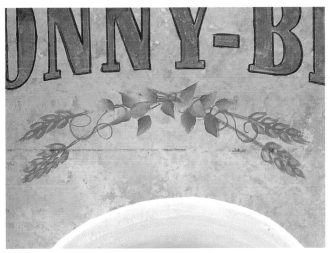

41 Paint little one-stroke leaves with Avocado and Yellow Ochre double loaded on a ¼-inch flat brush. Start on the chisel edge, push down, and lift back up to the chisel as you slide to the leaf tip.

42 Paint the flowers with Wedgewood Blue and Titanium White double loaded on a no. 3 round brush. These are five petal flowers. Using a no. 1 liner or your stylus, paint the dip-dot centers with Titanium White.

Finishing Touches

43 Sand the painting with a sanding sponge distressing the painting. You don't have to go over the face. Seal with DecoArt Acrylic Spray Sealer (Satin) and let dry.

44 Apply DecoArt Oak Gel Stain with a large foam brush, following the directions on the label.

45 Wipe off the stain with a clean, soft cloth.

46 Apply more stain on the edges and soften with a mop brush.

47 Apply the checkerboard detail with a small square sponge using Yellow Ochre over a Wedgewood Blue basecoat.

48 Apply eyelet lace trim, if you desire.

The Completed Basket Lid

If you can't find an old picnic basket, try using a new unfinished wooden tray.

The Completed Basket

From Plain Chest of Drawers to
Cape Hatteras Seascape

One of my favorite things to paint is this wonderful lighthouse, and I do so whenever I can. It takes me back to the summer vacation when I first visited North Carolina's "best-kept secret." That summer, my brother, sisters and I trekked to the top of this majestic lighthouse and looked out over the blue Atlantic and the miles of nearly deserted beach. It remains a wonderful memory.

To make this chest even more special, I added real shells. Can you guess where I gathered them? Yes, I kept them that long! Can you tell the real shells from the painted ones?

PROJECT

Seascape Patterns

These patterns may be hand-traced or photocopied for personal use only. Reduce at 83% to bring down to size.

Materials

PAINT: DecoArt Americana

 Americana Satins: Powder Blue

 Avocado

 Titanium White

 Slate Grey

 Black Green

 Prussian Blue

 Americana Satins: Honeycomb

 Hauser Dark Green

 Blue Haze

 Yellow Ochre

 Burnt Sienna

 Soft Black

 Americana Satins: Soft White

 Tomato Red

 Blue Violet

 Buttermilk

 Khaki Tan

 Raw Sienna

 Terra Cotta

 Red Iron Oxide

 Honey Brown

 Burnt Umber

 Sand

 Dark Chocolate

 Burnt Orange

 Graphite

Surface
- Wooden chest of drawers

Brushes
- 2-inch foam brush
- no. 2 mop
- ¼-inch dagger striper
- nos. 0 and 1 liners
- no. 2 fan or ½-inch rake
- ¼-inch and ½-inch flats
- ½-inch angle shader
- nos. 0 and 1 rounds
- medium scruffy brush

Additional Supplies
- Primer
- Painter's tape
- Brush 'n Blend Extender
- Sea sponge
- Toothbrush
- Carpenter's square
- Tape measure
- Pencil
- Seashells (optional)

Prepare the Surface

What an ugly little dresser this was! It had several layers of brown paint on it, but that was its only bad point. It was still sound and even had all the knobs. It was also small, which made it all the more versatile, and at thirty dollars it was another flea market bargain.

This chest of drawers was perfect for the seascape design I envisioned for it. What made it ideal was the front drawers that were flush. Other dressers may have protruding drawer facings that make painting more difficult.

The chest had to be stripped of its brown paint. The choice is yours whether you want to sand or strip a piece, but if you sand or strip it yourself, make sure you do it in a well-ventilated area, preferably outdoors.

Unfinished, Unprepped Surface

1 After stripping and sanding, prime the entire chest with a good stain-hiding primer. After the primer is dry, place the drawers back in the chest, but leave the knobs off until later.

With a pencil, lightly sketch a line around the chest where you want the horizon to be. I made mine just beneath the halfway point of the height of the piece. To make a straight horizon, measure down from the top of the chest and make a mark where you want the ocean to meet the sky. Move your tape measure around the chest and measure down, making marks about twelve-inches apart at the same height as the first mark. Then connect your marks horizontally with a straightedge or a level. Now sketch in rolling dunes just below the horizon line. There is no need to be an artist here. Just pull your pencil around the dresser, making a meandering line with long, subtle curves. You may even make the dunes peak above the horizon line, but only in a few places.

Paint the sky with Americana Satins Powder Blue down to your horizon line. Use a 2-inch foam brush to paint the body of the chest, but when you near the horizon line, switch to a smaller brush for accuracy. It's important that the horizon line be painted as straight as possible.

The areas between the lines on the dresser will be water. Basecoat it with Blue Haze using a ½-inch flat brush. Along the horizon line where the water meets the sky, float a mix of Blue Haze and Powder Blue (1:1). This will make the horizon appear far away.

Paint the sand with a mix of Americana Satins Soft White and Honeycomb (1:1). Use Soft White for highlights and more Honeycomb for darker sand and shading.

Begin the Seascape

2 Sponge on the clouds with a mix of Americana Satins Powder Blue + Titanium White (2:1) on a sea sponge.

3 Softly blend the sponging into the background with a mop brush.

4 On top of the previous cloud mix, sponge on Titanium White in a smaller area, staying mainly in the center. Again, softly blend with a mop brush.

5 Add the whitecaps with a ¼-inch dagger striper loaded with Titanium White. Use just the tip for the caps in the distance.

6 Spatter the bottom part of the sand with a spattering tool or toothbrush. Use Burnt Sienna, Avocado, Slate Grey and Buttermilk in this order.

The Trees

7 Add two parts Slate Grey to one part Black Green for the base mix. Load a no. 0 liner brush with this mix and paint the trunk and branches of the trees.

8 Shade the trees on the right side using the no. 0 liner brush loaded with the base mix plus a touch more Black Green.

9 Highlight the trees on the left side with the no. 0 liner brush loaded with the base mix plus a touch of Titanium White.

10 Add just enough Black Green to Avocado to darken the Avocado. Using a scruffy brush loaded with this mix, pounce at the branch ends.

11 Add a little Titanium White to Avocado to lighten it. Using a scruffy brush, pounce this mix on the left side of the tree to create foliage. Add more Titanium White to the Avocado mix to lighten it even further. Again, pounce on the left side, but in a smaller area.

The Grass and Fence

12 Using a no. 2 fan brush or ½-inch rake loaded with thinned Yellow Ochre, paint the distant grass.

13 Paint small clumps of grass with Avocado, Yellow Ochre and a touch of Raw Sienna all loaded on the brush at the same time.

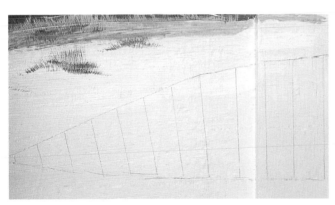

14 Sketch the guidelines for the fence by very lightly drawing a wedge shape. The bottom line should follow the contour of the sand. The upper line is a curved arch. Make vertical marks as guides for your fence posts. Give them a slight slant to give the illusion that the fence is leaning.

15 Mix Khaki Tan, Raw Sienna, Blue Violet and Slate Grey to make a blue-gray mix. Apply underneath the fence to make a shadow. Paint the fence pickets with Burnt Sienna using a ¼-inch flat brush.

16 Make the pickets smaller as if the fence were buried in the sand.

17 Shade the fence on the right side with a no. 0 liner loaded with Black Green and a touch of Burnt Sienna (enough to make it a brown color).

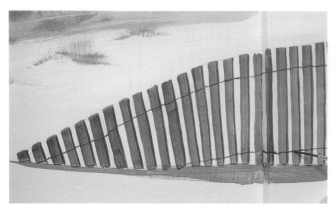

18 Add the wire with a no. 1 liner brush loaded with the fence shading color and a little more Black Green.

19 Add grass and sea oats in front of the fence. Start with Hauser Dark Green + Yellow Ochre (1:1) and scrub in the deepest shading using a ½-inch angle shader.

20 Using the same color loaded on a no. 0 liner brush, make long grasses. Add Burnt Sienna and more Yellow Ochre on the brush as you paint.

21 While the paint is still wet, pull out grass with the brush handle. With the dagger striper, go over some clumps to make longer grass blades.

22 Add the sea oats with a no. 1 round loaded with a mix of Yellow Ochre and Burnt Sienna. Create the tips of the sea oats with the same mix and a no. 0 round.

The Cape Hatteras
Lighthouse

24 Paint the light element with Graphite and Titanium White in varying shades. Use a liner brush to indicate the individual panes of glass.

23 Decide how large you want the lighthouse. This will depend on the size of the dresser. Since the lighthouse is the focal point of the artwork, it should be as large as you can make it, providing that the top is about six inches from the top of the dresser and the base is below the horizon line. This will sufficiently "plant" the lighthouse beyond the dunes, and it will appear as if it is sitting on the land.

Use a carpenter's square to line up the vertical dotted line on the pattern shown on page 128. This will ensure that the lighthouse is straight up and down. Secure the pattern in place with painter's tape and leave one side open. Slide the tracing paper under the pattern and transfer the design.

25 Paint the observation deck with a ¼-inch flat brush loaded with Soft Black. Use a no. 0 liner brush for the smaller linework.

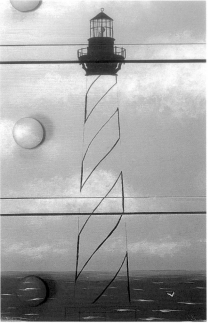

26 Outline the black stripe with Soft Black using a no. 1 liner brush. These are your guidelines.

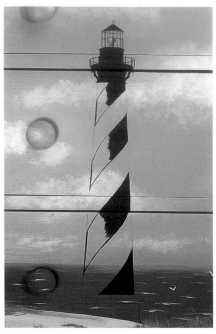

27 Paint the right side of the black stripes with Soft Black.

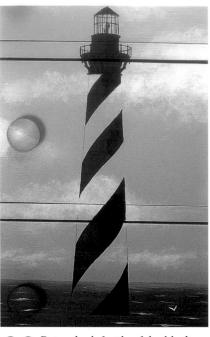

28 Paint the left side of the black stripes with Graphite and blend where the colors meet. Highlight the left side of the observation deck with Graphite.

29 Mix Slate Grey, Graphite and Titanium White for a sharp highlight. Use extender with this mix to blend into the black background.

30 Paint the shaded side of the white stripe with Slate Grey using a ¼-inch flat.

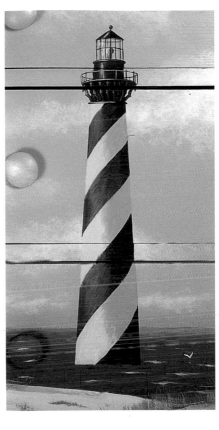

30 Undercoat the left side of the white stripes with a mix of Titanium White and Slate Grey. Use Brush 'n Blend to blend the mix into the shaded areas.

32 Apply Titanium White on the far left of the white stripes. Blend into the background with Brush 'n Blend.

33 Undercoat the lighthouse's base with Yellow Ochre. Lightly float Slate Grey on the left side of the white stripe. On the right side of the white stripe and the left side of the black stripe, float a mix of Slate Grey and Soft Black (2:1).

34 Reapply the pattern details for the base.

35 Paint the red brick with Burnt Orange on the lightest side, Burnt Sienna on the front, and Burnt Sienna + Dark Chocolate (1:1) on the shadow side. Edge the bricks on the front with Khaki Tan.

36 Paint the brick trim with Khaki Tan and Titanium White on the far left section, Khaki Tan and Dark Chocolate on the third section, and straight Dark Chocolate on the last section.

37 Shade the individual bricks and underneath the pediments with Dark Chocolate loaded on a no. 0 liner brush.

38 Highlight the individual bricks with Khaki Tan and Titanium White loaded on a no. 0 liner brush.

The Shells and Starfish

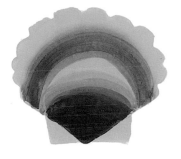  

Shells

1. Basecoat with Mocha. Add arched lines with thinned Dark Chocolate. Add the triangle at the base with Dark Chocolate.

2. Blend into the wet Dark Chocolate with Red Iron Oxide and Titanium White. Allow the Red Iron Oxide to dry first.

3. Add deep lines of Dark Chocolate and Red Iron Oxide. Shade with Dark Chocolate. Add detail lines and highlight grooves with Titanium White.

Starfish

1. Basecoat with Honey Brown. Float Burnt Umber shading on the edges.

2. Stipple on rows of dots with Dark Chocolate.

3. Dot with Yellow Ochre. Highlight with Sand, then Titanium White.

39 If you desire, you can glue real shells onto your piece instead of painting them. Simply apply a shadow underneath and you won't be able to tell the real ones from the painted ones.

40 This will certainly fool the eye! It is a fake shadow, but a real shell.

Detail of the Left Side

Detail of the Right Side

The Completed Chest of Drawers, Front

Close-Up of the Lighthouse

Resources

Robert Simmons Expressions Brushes:

Daler-Rowney, U.S.A.
2 Corporate Drive
Cranbury NJ 08512
(609) 655-5252

Americana Acrylic Paints, Mediums and Finishes:

DecoArt
P.O. Box 360
Stanford KY 40484
(800) 367-3047

In Canada:

Crafts Canada
2745 29th St. N.E.
Calgary, ON
T1Y 7B5

Mercury Art & Craft Supershop
332 Wellington St.
London, ON
N6C 4P7
(519) 434-1636

Town & Country Folk Art Supplies
93 Green Lane
Thornhill, ON
L3T 6K6
(905) 882-0199

Maureen McNaughton Enterprises
RR #2
Bellwood, ON
N0B 1J0
(519) 843-5648

Folk Art Enterprises
P.O.Box 1088
Ridgetown, ON / N0P 2C0
(888) 214-0062

MacPherson Craft Wholesale
83 Queen St. E.
P.O. Box 1870
St. Mary's, ON / N4X 1C2
(519) 284-1741

Wooden Tray for Bonny-Blu project:

Boulder Hill Woodworks
HC 61, P.O. Box 1036
St. George, ME 04857
(800) 448-4891

Pine Arch Clock for Faux Delft Tile project:

Walnut Hollow Farm Woodcraft Store
1409 State Rd. 23
Dodgeville, WI 53533
(800) 950-5101

Metric Conversion Chart

to convert	to	multiply by
Inches	Centimeters	2.54
Centimeters	Inches	0.4
Feet	Centimeters	30.5
Centimeters	Feet	0.03
Yards	Meters	0.9
Meters	Yards	1.1
Sq. Inches	Sq. Centimeters	6.45
Sq. Centimeters	Sq. Inches	0.16
Sq. Feet	Sq. Meters	0.09
Sq. Meters	Sq. Feet	10.8
Sq. Yards	Sq. Meters	0.8
Sq. Meters	Sq. Yards	1.2
Pounds	Kilograms	0.45
Kilograms	Pounds	2.2
Ounces	Grams	28.4
Grams	Ounces	0.04

Index

Explore Decorative Painting with North Light Books

In this inspiring guide, Donna Dewberry shows you how to paint 10 all-new projects designed especially for furniture. You'll transform old and new shelves, tables, chests and cabinets into treasured objects that complement the décor of every room.

From soft florals and meandering vines to ripe cherries and delicate china, you'll master each project with clear, step-by-step instructions that detail every stroke.

1-58180-016-9, paperback, 128 pages

If you're high on enthusiasm but low on patience, here's the book for you! Inside you'll find everything you need to create inexpensive, personalized gifts and beautiful accessories for your home in no time flat!

Hundreds of illustrated steps show simple ways to paint favorite flowers, fruits and berries on inexpensive items, such as wooden spoons, candy jars and baskets. It's easy!

0-89134-990-1, paperback, 128 pages

Start with an old or unfinished piece of furniture, add in a little acrylic paint and Kerry Trout's clever motifs, and you've got the makings of a handpainted masterpiece!

This book provides nine step-by-step projects and an exciting array of realistic scenes and trompe l'oeil effects. Kerry covers everything from preparing your surface to giving your piece that authentic, antique look. It's packed with full-color photos and clear instructions!

0-89134-980-4, paperback, 128 pages